GW01403385

A Cardinal's Song

By Kate Bria

Illustrated by Elsa Linsky

Copyright © 2024 by Kate Bria

All rights reserved. No part of this publication may be reproduced, distributed, or transmitted in any form or by any means, including photocopying, recording, or other electronic or mechanical methods, without prior written permission from the publisher.

THIS BOOK BELONGS TO:

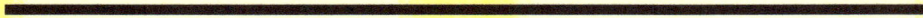

_____

_____

A little girl and her mother walked down the lane in their neighborhood. They saw flowers and trees and bees. They also heard a cardinal sing.

The little girl's mother said, "That's a cardinal, honey. Can you see its red wings?"

They both looked up and saw the bold, beautiful red cardinal. Its red feathers beamed vibrantly in the sunlight. The mother said to her daughter, "Cardinals appear when angels are near, so never fear, for your loved ones are always here."

Years passed, and the little girl grew up and moved away to a big city. There were still flowers, trees, and bees, but not as many as there used to be.

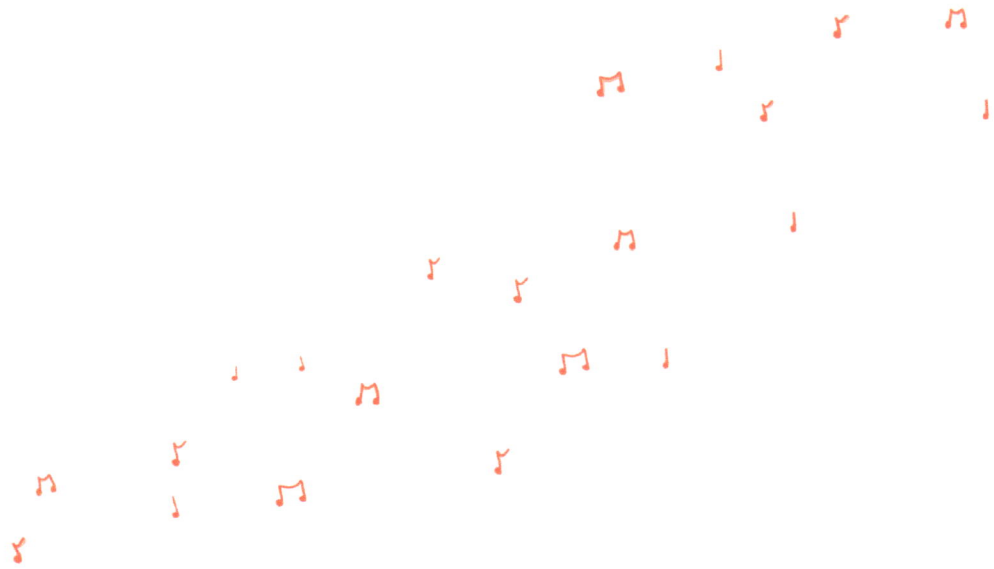

One day, when she was having a sad time, she heard something that sounded oh so divine. A sweet melody floated through the air, drawing her attention to the window. There, perched in a tree, was a red cardinal.

As she listened to the cardinal's song, she was filled with peace. She heard her mother's voice saying, "Cardinals appear when angels are near, so never fear, for your loved ones are always here."

Seeing the cardinal, the girl smiled, and she
thought of her mother and called her.

As they talked to each other, the weight of their troubles seemed to lighten.
They both found a sense of healing in a Cardinal's song.

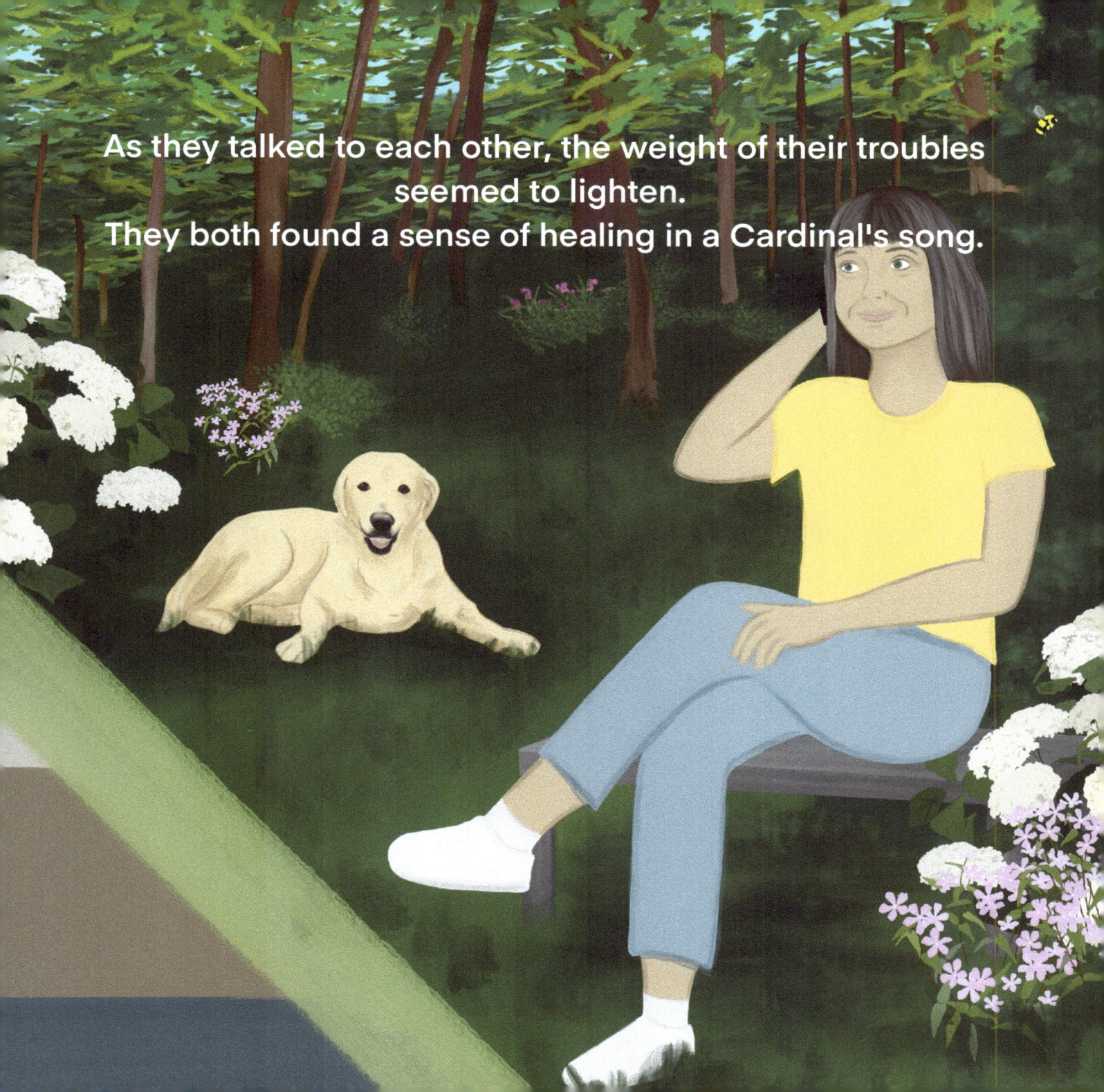

As time went on, and the seasons changed, so did
many other things.
The girl now had a family of her own, with two
beautiful daughters.
There were still walks with flowers, trees, and bees.
But her mother was no longer there to see.

Now when she heard a cardinal's call, she knew it was her mother saying,
"I am really not far at all."

One day in early spring, as she sat outside with her
daughters, she heard a familiar
sound. A bird's song that was so profound.
Like a warm hug from up above, a cardinal appeared.
And she knew it
was someone dear who was near.
She said to her daughters, "Cardinals appear when
angels are near, so never fear, for
your grandmother is always here."

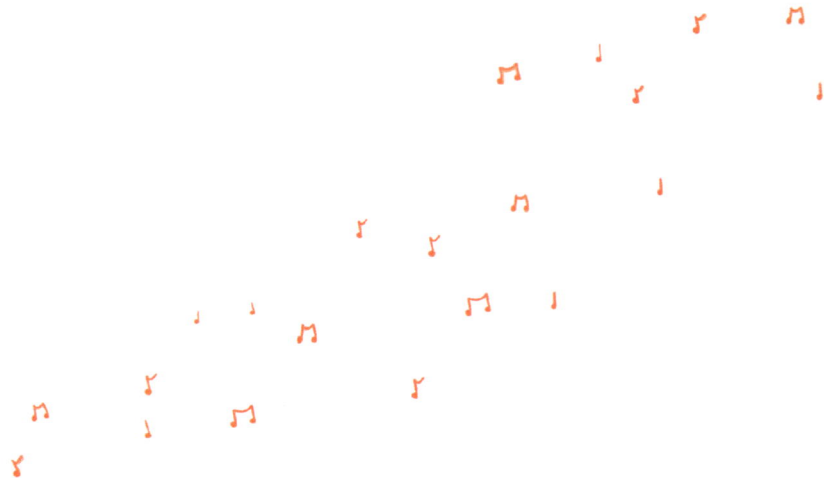

Dedicated to My Mom. I am always looking up.

Milton Keynes UK
Ingram Content Group UK Ltd.
UKHW051555011224
451618UK00029B/15

9 798218 548407